Dr. Paul Reeve: The Complete Interview on the Ban

(Note this conversation was recorded on January 18, 2017 in Salt Lake City, Utah. I will use GT for Gospel Tangents to indicate when I am talking to Paul. The interview has been lightly edited to remove verbal miscues and to arrange the history in a chronological order.)

Introduction

Gospel Tangents needs your support. Please consider donating to our website, https://GospelTangents.com in any amount. We will use your donation, and the information from these podcasts to produce professional Mormon History Documentaries and other resources such as this.

Rick Bennett of Gospel Tangents sat down with Dr. Paul Reeve, history professor at the University of Utah to discuss findings from his recent book Religion of a Different Color which discusses the history of the racial ban by the Church of Jesus Christ of Latter-day Saints between the 1840s to 1978. Transcripts of the interviews were previous published as a series of interviews. This edition combines the entire 90 minute interviews.

Table of Contents

Introduction

Part 1 – **How Mormons Became a Racial Category**

Part 2 – **How did Others Deal with Slavery?**

Part 3 – **How did Joseph Deal with Muslims?** (and Chinese and Indians?)

Part 4 – **The Black Mormon Scandals** – events leading to the LDS priesthood/temple ban

Part 5 – **Becoming a Fanboy of Orson Pratt** (the Apostle)

Part 6 – **Dating the LDS Temple & Priesthood Ban**

Part 7 – **Dr. Reeve's Modern Lessons**

Epilogue

Additional Resources

The Interview

How Mormons Became a Racial Category

GT: Welcome to Gospel Tangents Podcast. I'm here with historian and author Paul Reeve here at the University of Utah. I appreciate you allowing us to come and let us talk to you today here Paul. Thanks.

Paul: Thank you, thanks for the opportunity.

GT: Paul is the author of the book Religion of a Different Color. I wanted to talk a little bit about the book. Before I do that, do you have any other books in the works right now?

Paul: I'm working on a documentary history of the 1852 Utah Territorial Legislature.

GT: Oh!

Paul: It's the territorial legislature that Brigham Young speaks to, and it's the first known articulation of the prophet/president of the LDS Church of a race-based priesthood restriction and it's within that context of the legislative debates taking place. [I'm] working with LaJean Carruth who has transcribed the speeches from that legislative session from their original Pitman shorthand. Some of them have never been transcribed since 1852 and Christopher Rich who is a legal scholar, the three of us are working on a documentary history of that legislative session.

GT: That's exciting, because I actually wanted to talk to you about that today as well. We'll go into a little bit more history there. I did not know that. That's exciting. Paul, you are a—well, as I recall you had a recent promotion.

Paul: That's right.

GT: Can you tell us about that?

Paul: I was promoted from associate professor to full professor this academic year, July 2016. [There are] three levels of professors. Most people aren't aware, but three levels of professors in academia: assistant professor, associate professor, and full professor. I was promoted to full professor.

GT: You're also the director of graduate studies I understand.

Paul: That's correct.

GT: That's a pretty time-consuming thing I guess right now?

Paul: It is time-consuming. We're in the middle of the admissions process and so we get to decide who gets admitted and who doesn't, as well as financial aid and so it's just generally keeping track of graduate students.

GT: Yeah, well I understand. I really appreciate you taking some time out to talk to us.

Paul: It's my pleasure.

GT: Well let's talk a little bit about your book, Religion of a Different Color. It's kind of an interesting take on that. Kind of the premise of the book, although correct me if I am wrong, is that Mormons were once too white, and now we're not white enough, so I'd kind of like to talk a little bit about the evolution of that. Can you talk about that a little bit?

Paul: Sure, so just to be clear, the exact opposite of what you said: not white enough in the 19th century, and then by the 21st century too white.

GT: Oh yes. That's what I meant.

Paul: So that's the basic arc of the trajectory of the argument for the book, so in the 19th century Mormonism was actually born into a very charged racial context. Even immigrants from northern and western Europe were being racialized as not fully white. There was a racial hierarchy that animated 19th century thought about where people fit in, and Anglo-Saxons were at the top of that hierarchy, and then Irish immigrants or Italian immigrants were seen as less than fully white somewhere down that racial ladder, and obviously you have Native Americans, Asians, African Americans at the bottom of the racial ladder, and 19th century observers were trying to figure out where to situate Mormons.

The argument of the book is that they weren't merely religiously suspect but also racially suspect. You had medical doctors who actually argued that Mormonism, Mormon polygamy in particular was giving rise to a new race, a degraded, sunken, degenerate race and therefore Mormons and their bodies were denigrated as not white. Really if you take the argument to the extent that it's taken in the 19th century, what's at stake in the minds of outside observers is American democracy. John C. Calhoun says on the floor of the United States Senate, democracy is the government of white race. The fear was that in practicing polygamy, as well as giving their free will over the despots Joseph Smith and Brigham Young, as outsiders viewed it, Mormons were actually reverting away from civilization, backwards into barbarism, and into savagery, and therefore democracy is at stake.

GT: Hmmm. I think that's kind of a strange thing for us to think about, that Italians were a different race, Europeans were a different race. How did they come about these ideas?

Paul: It's a really good question. I think that what's important to keep in mind that it's a very fluid and illogical racial context in the 19th century. You have a variety of different thinkers kind of suggesting ideas about what race means. In the 19th century a nation could also equal a race, the Irish race was commonly referred to in the 19th century. Celts, what we would consider different ethnic groups today were considered different racial groups. Thinkers in the 19th century are simply trying to make sense of these various groups of people and try to create a racial hierarchy and in their mind, whiteness equals freedom, blackness equals slavery, and then you have this gradation in between. Where do you situate everyone else?

That helps you to determine how they're treated, access to social/political and economic power are bound up in where you're situated on this racial hierarchy, and so the racialization for Mormons starts before they are openly practicing polygamy, but polygamy gives it simply a new life, especially after Mormons openly practice polygamy. The argument is that we have this fearful decline away from civilization backwards into barbarism. The development theory is in operation in the 19th century. It simply posited that all societies go through three basic phases: they develop from savagery into barbarism, and then from barbarism into civilization. Once you arrive at civilization, you have shed markers of barbarism and savagery, and a couple of those markers were polygamy and adherence to despotic rule.

With Mormons, the fear was, these are people who might look white, right, but they're not behaving the way that white people are supposed to behave. They are practicing polygamy and giving their free will over to despots, and therefore the fear was you have this slippage backwards from civilization back into barbarism and into savagery.

GT: It seems like their kind of combining some sociology with race and creating a strange definition.

Paul: Yes. Absolutely. Absolutely. So people are just sort of casting about, trying to figure out what it means to be white or less than white, what it means to be black, what it means to be Native American. Religious thinkers long looked to the Bible to understand where the races came from, and they would like to Noah's sons after the flood: Shem, Ham, and Japheth and argue that those three sons give rise to Europeans, Africans, and Asians, the three major groups. But you have what we would consider pseudo-scientists today, but in the 19th century people who are arguing that in fact that there was more than one genesis, or more than one origin, that the races were so distinct, black and white were so distinct that there must have been separate species. It's called the polygenesis theory, more than one genesis.

Religious thinkers rejected it because they saw it as an attack against the Bible. The Bible only talks about one creation. The polygenesis theory suggests there must be more than one creation, giving rise to separate races that were so distinct that they were different species. So religious thinkers rejected that because they said it attacks the Bible, so Joseph Smith and Brigham Young for example rejected the argument of polygenesis and said we all come from one origin, right? But then especially with Brigham Young he'll start to argue that, how do you account for blackness? He uses the Curse of Cain in the Bible that predates even the founding of Mormonism by 1000 years. That's part of the broader Judeo-Christian tradition that's traceable to the Old Testament.

GT: Ok, that brings up a few questions. So Brigham Young pushes it back instead of the Curse of Ham, he pushes it 1000 years beyond to the Curse of Cain. Wow, I hadn't realized that. That's kind of interesting. That's a development that Brigham Young did that most Protestants didn't do. They would have just referred to the Curse of Ham?

Paul: Well, both of them are in operation. The Curse of Cain predates Mormonism as well. Genesis says God put a mark on Cain and his descendants, and the idea that the mark was black skin predates Mormonism by 1000 years. The earliest references are Jewish scribes and it becomes a part of the broader Judeo-Christian that is passed down in the West over almost 1000 years, and it's in existence before Mormonism is even founded. There's a black slave, I think he's writing in 1828 or 29, he writes a narrative and he says white people are just ready to tell me that I am the descendant of Cain and I am cursed, and that's a couple of years before Mormonism is founded in 1830 and like I said, there have been some studies of those notions in the broader Judeo-Christian tradition looking way back in European history, sort of the Jewish glosses on the Bible. They are the ones who are suggesting that the mark that God put on Cain and his descendants is the black skin. It becomes part of this broader Judeo-Christian that Brigham Young would have been immersed in. Joseph Smith does talk about the Curse of Ham, but it is Brigham Young gives life to the Curse of Cain and associates it with a priesthood restriction.

GT: Oh that's really interesting. I wanted to just loop back around and talk a little bit about this polygenesis theory, that was kind of interesting to me. Going back to that, essentially they were saying there was a white Adam and Eve, a black Adam and Eve, an Asian Adam and Eve, and that kind of a thing?

Paul agrees: Um, Hmm.

GT: I mean obviously where would they get thieIrish Adam and Eve? Some of these other race things don't really make a lot of sense.

Paul: Yeah they hadn't really fully kind of worked that out. The polygenesis group—mostly black versus white, right? But suggesting that the races are so distinct that there must have been separate origins, separate creations. {Paul shrugs his shoulders}. You know, it's just simply their effort at trying to account for the distinction between the races, and like I said, religious thinkers reject it because they see it as an attack on the Bible, the creation narrative in the Bible.

GT: That's interesting. I remember one of your presentations at the Mormon History Association, you talked about some pseudo-sciences, physiognomy, I think, where you could look at a Mormon, and he had beady eyes, and you could know that he was a Mormon, or something like that. Can you talk a little bit more about that?

Paul: Sure. Physiognomy, as well as phrenology, are two pseudo-sciences in the 19th century and both of them turn their attention to the Mormons. Physiognomy is the study of this notion that you could read a person's character traits through his or her face and one of the ways in which they attempted to read the Mormon face was through the eyes. They actually used an illustration of Brigham Young to suggest that he had poly-erotic eyes versus Margaret Fuller Ossoli who was a 19th century feminist who was so devoted, the story goes, to her lover that when their ship sinks, she had a chance to save herself but would rather drown with her lover than live without him. That's the example of mono-erotic eyes.

The illustration in the book is of her eyes in comparison to Brigham Young's eyes. She had really wide, round eyes like a dove that mates for life. Brigham Young had eyes, at least in the depiction, it's just an artist's drawing but has eyes that are very narrow and kind of closed, and those were deemed poly-erotic eyes similar to a hog which mates with whoever it wants to. Those were the ways in which there was an effort at reading Mormon faces.

Phrenologists also played up the distinctions amongst Mormons. Joseph Smith had his skull read by Phrenologists and other Mormon leaders did as well and the suggestion was there was something distinct that sets Mormons apart. It's physical, not just religious in other words, right? It's really by the 1840s that outsiders are referring to a Mormon race and you have medical doctors who visit Utah Territory who suggest that there is a new race emerging out of the Great Basin. There's actually a conference held at the New Orleans Academy of Sciences in 1860 where medical doctors gather and they have a conference about the supposed new race that's emerging in the Great Basin. All the doctors present at the conference buy the argument and actually push it forward except for one. One doctor argues against that. He simply says that, Look, it's only been thirty years since this religion has been around. We should really engage in an empirical study for thirty more years before we can conclusively say that Mormonism is giving rise to a new race. Everyone else just simply said that polygamy because it's degraded, is producing degraded offspring. Therefore a new race is emerging in the Great Basin.

They actually argue that Mormonism would solve itself if the United States could stem the tide of outside converts, converts from Europe. It would produce sterility in the next generation because it's degraded. The next generation, within a few generations, men are going to become sterile and it will die out of its own force, if they could simply stop immigrants from coming in from Europe and bringing new blood in. That would perpetuate the problem much further into the future.

GT: Wow. These are some strange ideas.

Paul: They are very strange ideas.

GT: It makes you wonder what are our strange ideas that in 100 years people will go, I can't believe they thought that!

Paul: Exactly.

{both chuckle}

GT: I have heard the thought that there are some people that say, black-white DNA, it's 96 or 98% exactly the same and race should be a sociological term. Even today they say that, instead of there's some sort of a physical difference. Yeah we've got black skin, white skin, I guess yellow skin with Asians, but what are your thoughts about that? Is that something we should just do away with race declarations altogether? What do you think?

Paul: Well I think one of the conclusions from the book, if you can racialize Mormons then you can racialize anyone. It really points to the fact that race is not a biological reality, it's a social construct. In other words we've used it in society to differentiate between different groups. It's important to simply understand that. I don't know that we'll ever get rid of its sociological function, but it's important to understand it's not a biological reality like you mentioned, right? The bulk of our DNA is actually the same. Black people have more melanin in their skin. End of story, that's it, right?

From DNA studies, we actually all are Africans. That's one of the conclusions DNA has taught us is that origin of man comes from Africa. Really we all start from Africa. It's all sort of evolutionary biology after that in terms of where people spread, and exposure to the sun, lighter skin versus darker skin. Any notion that there is biological distinction is completely false. Race just functions as a social construct and I think the book bears that out. White people, people who are predominantly white, like Mormons in the 19th century can be viewed or constructed, *imagined*, as a completely different race, it just points to the lie of race as anything but a social construct.

GT: Well that's very interesting. I'm going to give you a little bit of my background. I have a masters degree in Statistics, here from the University of Utah, a Utah man I am!

Paul chuckles: Yay! Yes!

GT: In some of my epidemiology classes I had, they've said there are always three variables you should always consider in any study: sex, race, and age, because generally there are differences between all three of those. Older people are different than younger people, men are different than women, and we always include race. There does seem to be some issues, and I don't know if those are sociological or physical.

For example, blacks generally do not survive heart attacks as well as whites. Now the question is, why? Is there something biological about blacks that is the case, or is it more an issue that blacks have an issue of worse insurance? Race is more of a placeholder for economic status. It's kind of interesting. I don't know that anybody has been able to answer that. From an epidemiological point of view, we always want to keep that in there because it means something.

Paul: Sure.

GT: Whether it's biological or sociological or economic, that's subject to debate, but that's something that's very important I know in medical studies.

Paul: Sure. Yeah. So when I talk about it as a social construct, talking about the way in which it functions in society in terms of access to political, social, economic power, and in those ways, it's the way we have constructed, *you're not worthy of citizenship within the United States because your skin's color is different than mine.* The very first Congress , [17]90, establishes conditions for how you can naturalize as a citizen. You have to be free and white. That's a social construct regarding race. Somehow people who are less than white are incapable of democracy. That's the argument Congress is making, the argument that the Supreme Court makes. In those kind of ways, race is functioning to distinguish between white and black and actually elevate whites over blacks and disadvantage one group over the other only out of the social construct, not out of any biological fact that black people are incapable of democracy.

How Did Others Deal with Slavery?

GT: Let's talk a little bit about Missouri. I believe it was W.W. Phelps back in 1832 if my memory is correct. There's an article in the newspaper, you could probably tell me what it is.

Paul: The Messenger and Advocate

GT: Ok, and so that caused a lot of stir. Can you talk a little bit about what happened there?

Paul: Sure. [W.W.] Phelps publishes an article titled *Free People of Color* in Jackson County, Missouri. It simply is an announcement that after Jackson County has been defined by Joseph Smith as the gathering place, as the New Zion. Phelps is concerned about black Latter-day Saints, so he writes this article *Free People of Color*. He simply says, Look. If my fellow black Latter-day Saints are going to gather to Zion, Jackson County, you need to be aware that this is slave territory and here are two aspects of the Missouri legal code that will govern your life if you immigrate to Missouri. He simply quotes from the legal code, tells black Mormons that if they immigrate, they need to make sure they have papers substantiating their free status; otherwise they will be subject to being whipped and expelled from the state of Missouri. He doesn't want that to happen to his co-religionists. He says, as long as we have no special rule in this church as to people of color, let prudence guide. Just be aware that if you're going to immigrate to Missouri, it's a slave state and there are going to be rules that will govern your ability to move about freely in a state and I don't want you to run afoul of the law, so here are the sections of the legal code in Missouri that will govern your behavior.

Outsiders, non-Mormons in Missouri read that article and get up in arms really quickly. They suggest that the Mormons are inviting free blacks to the state of Missouri to incite a slave rebellion. Beyond that they also argue they are inviting free blacks to the state of Missouri to steal our white wives and daughters. Fear of race mixing is always bound up in these charges leveled against the Mormons almost from the beginning, that somehow they are inciting a slave rebellion is one argument, but also race mixing was the other argument. You're inviting free blacks, and black men. There was the myth of the black beast rapist that animates white people's concerns of who black people are, especially black men. All black men just simply want white women, and that charge is leveled against the Mormons.

Before the incident plays out, Phelps will issue an *Extra* Edition where he tries to calm the fears of the Missourians. They don't buy it. They simply say we don't buy anything you've said in your *Extra*. We know really what you're intending to do. You're intending to invite blacks here to start a race riot. They will attack his printing office; they'll scatter his press into the street. His printing office and his home were the same basic building. They destroy it. They completely level it. They drag two men, Bishop James Allen and another man into town square and tar and feather them.

GT: Bishop Partridge I believe.

Paul: Bishop Partridge, there you go. James Allen and Bishop Partridge, that's right. That begins the expulsion of the Mormons from Jackson County.

GT: So Mormons really have a complicated history. Let's talk a little bit about Kirtland. A really interesting thing to me was Mormons, it sounds like, tried to walk this really thin line where they were against slavery but they were also against the Abolitionist movement. I wonder if you could talk a little bit about that.

Paul: Sure. It's really important to have maybe a more nuanced understanding of what it meant to be an abolitionist in the 19th century. There are various degrees of being a member of an anti-slavery institution in the antebellum period. The majority position is a Colonization Position. In the minds of the white majority that were against slavery, slavery presented a two-fold problem. It presented a problem because it violated the founding principles articulated in the Declaration of Independence, that all men are created equal, and this sense that we shouldn't enslave anyone.

It's a problem because we have an unfree population. But the second part of the problem is a racial problem. Just because they're against slavery doesn't mean that they are in favor of racial equality. They're simply against slavery and then once you free the slaves, what do you do with them? You certainly don't want them moving north and living amongst white people; once again the fear that they are going to engage in race mixing. So the majority position favors actually sending the free black population to Africa. It's called the Colonization Position.

[In] 1830, you have a radical new group of immediate abolitionists who start to argue—William Roy Garrison is leading this group. He founds the *Liberator*, a newspaper where he starts to argue for immediate abolitionism and full racial equality. This will touch off anti-abolitionist riots across the north because the white majority, once again, doesn't want black people living amongst them. They may be against slavery but they are not in favor of full racial equality.

That's the difficult racial waters that Mormonism finds itself immersed in. When Mormons are labeled as abolitionists who are in favor of amalgamation—amalgamation is the pre-Civil War term for race mixing, then Joseph Smith finds it politically expedient to speak out against the immediate abolitionists and amalgamation, race mixing. He does so in 1836 in this very charged racial context where Mormons have already been expelled from Jackson County because of the fear that they are inciting a slave rebellion and in favor of race mixing. He speaks in 1836, he speaks out against the immediate abolitionists and against race mixing as well. It's important to immerse it within that broader context for it to make sense.

GT: So I'm trying to see if we can come up with maybe a modern-day equivalent. Abortion seems to be kind of a hot button issue. You've got abortion bombers on the one side, and you've got pro-[choice] people on the other side: a woman should be able to have an abortion any time they want. I do believe that the [Mormon] Church even today, once again is trying to walk a little bit of a middle line in the fact that, well, we'll allow abortion in the case of a rape or to save the life of a mother. Would you say that that's kind of a similar thing as to what the church was trying to do in the 1830s and 40s?

Paul: Yeah, that might work as an analogy. I mean if you go with the church's position on abortion in the 21st century, abortion has to be legal for its position to be valid, right? They simply would like to restrict it to rape, incest, or the health of the mother, but nonetheless it would have to be legal for that to happen, right? So marking out more of a middle ground, probably more to the right of the middle ground, but more of a middle ground amongst those polarizing positions other people have staked out.

I think Joseph Smith is attempting to do so in 1836. The interesting thing is that almost every protestant denomination in the 19th century also speaks out against the radical abolitionists and against amalgamation. So they're all speaking out: Presbyterians, Methodists, even the Quakers denounce radical abolitionists. Quakers are in favor of gradual emancipation. They're against slavery, but what's the process for doing it? They are also fearful of the immediate abolitionists and the anti-abolitionist backlash and they also come out against the immediate abolitionism. It situates Joseph Smith I think within a bigger context where religious leaders are fearful of the immediate abolitionist movement, and Joseph Smith is right on with the rest of those religious groups.

Joseph Smith actually stakes out a really open perspective in terms of who's allowed within Mormonism and to become a preacher within Mormonism. You have the Methodists, the Presbyterians, and the Baptists will either split or experience schisms over those questions. Mormonism actually allows white slaveholders and black slaves to be baptized and into their religious kingdom, abolitionists, and anti-abolitionists. They are casting a wide net in terms of who they are accepting within the bounds of Mormonism. Those questions are causing schisms or splits within Methodism, Presbyterians, and Baptists.

GT: Since you mentioned the splits, especially with Methodism, I served a mission in South Carolina so I was very familiar with the A.M.E. Churches. A.M.E. stands for African Methodist Episcopal. (I always thought, how did Methodist and Episcopal get together?) Is that a result of these schisms you're talking about where the black Methodists went to the A.M.E. Churches, and the whites stayed as regular Methodists?

Paul: I wish I was more up to speed on all the various different groups. I don't think that AME is actually a result of this split. The Southern Methodists are a result of this split. There's a split between Southern and Northern

Methodists, Southern Baptists are a result of this split, and then there's a schism within the Presbyterians.

GT: Southern Methodists are white, and Southern Baptists are white, and how does that...?

Paul: No it's just a question of, will you allow slaveholders as preachers or as missionaries in your ordination? Southern Baptists, for example, were arguing of course we will. Northern Baptists were saying No. They should be forbidden.

GT: This wasn't a racial division so much as just what's your position?

Paul: Right. What's your position on the questions of the day, vis a vis, slavery? Who are you going to allow to be a missionary or a preacher? Can a slaveholder become a preacher in your group? Southerners said yeah, of course they should be allowed to. Northerners rejected that and it caused a split of Southern Baptists.

GT: So it was a split among whites, not a white versus a black?

Paul: Correct, correct, based on questions about slavery, and racial issues. Segregation within these churches was par for the course. If you're going to allow slaves, they're going to have segregated worship. More often than not, that's what would lead to them forming their own congregations, so the A.M.E. for their own worship purposes because they're not allowed full equality, a lot of times within the mainstream churches.

So Mormonism avoids that split altogether simply by casting a wide net and allowing black slaves, white slave masters, free blacks, former slaves, abolitionists, anti-abolitionists. These are the political positions of the day that at least initially were independent of their Mormonism.

But eventually, those questions will also have to be resolved within the fold and that takes place in 1852 in Utah Territory.

What were Joseph Smith's views on Muslims, Chinese, and Indians?

GT: Let's talk a little bit about Nauvoo. I know there was a letter written in 1840s where I believe it was the city council, though correct me if I'm wrong, that welcomed the Mohammedans, or what we would today call Muslims. As you talked about that, it seems that Mormons were very accepting of all people, blacks, whites, slave owners, non-slave owners. That was another reason why the rest of white America didn't like Mormons. Talk about how accepting Mormons were, especially of Muslims, blacks, and even Indians and Chinese.

Paul: Right. Yeah so that was one of the things that caused the Mormons problems especially in the first 20 years or so of Mormonism. They were branded as being too accepting of people that the rest of white America knew should be segregated or even enslaved. Accusations leveled against them in the 1830s up through the 1840s, they had opened up an asylum for rogues, vagabonds, and free blacks. Missionaries preaching in the south were accused of conspiring with Indians and walking out with colored women. In Missouri they were charged with actually promoting black ascendancy over whites, that they would elevate blacks above whites. That's how open they were.

There's actually a British officer, Edward Strutt Abdy, who's on tour of the United States in the 1830s from Britain. He's here to study American institutions and he returns back to Britain and he writes a three volume book about his journey in America and in this three volume book he actually says, he comes across a copy of the Book of Mormon, produced by this new religious sect in America and he reads it. He actually points out verses in 2 Nephi

26 where it says 'all are alike unto God, black and white.' He said Mormons have this radical vision of racial equality, and it's going to get them in trouble, especially in the state of Missouri. That's how radical their vision is. He points to the Book of Mormon as evidence of this and says, they're not going to last long because of their open racial vision.

So those are the accusations leveled against them by outsiders. That's one of the things I tried to do in the book [Religion of a Different Color] was, a lot of times the Mormon racial story has been told only from the inside perspective and I was interested in, well, what are outsiders saying about who Mormon are and how they behave racially. It was really fascinating to then come across these accusations being leveled against the Mormons that they are too open, too inviting of all people.

Like you mentioned in Nauvoo when they write their vision of religious equality, they simply say everyone's welcome to worship in Nauvoo. We don't discriminate. There's no religious discrimination and there's a whole long list of Christian denominations that are welcome in Nauvoo. The only non-Christian group mentioned were Muslims, and they simply say yeah we welcome Muslims here as well. So Joseph Smith was branded as an American Mohammad very early on in his religious career yet he is open and accepting of into his religious community in Nauvoo and simply says religious freedom should be for everyone. An attack against religious liberty against one group is an attack against all groups, so we should be at the forefront defending religious freedom and religious liberty.

GT: That's cool. In your book I think you spent a chapter both on Native Americans as well as on Chinese. Can you tell us the comments from outsiders that had problems with those two groups?

Paul: Sure. Obviously Mormons have a bit of a theological, distinct understanding of who Native Americans are, fallen descendants of ancient Israel. Mormonism is founded in 1830, the same year that the United States passes the Indian Removal Act which simply stipulates that Native Americans east of the Mississippi are to be rounded up and removed to Indian Country designated west of the Mississippi. That's supposed to solve the Indian problem, simply round them up, get them out of the way of white settlements and let whites simply fill in the land where the Native Americans had been living.

So that's what's going on in the U.S., and then Mormonism comes along and says well we have a new book of scripture and it purports to be a history of this group of people. They actually have a divine destiny, and this does not set well with a lot of the American population. Mormons will be accused of conspiring with Indians against true, white Americans, with intermarriage amongst them which they in fact do engage in. They have no problem intermarrying amongst the Indians. By the time they arrive in Utah Territory, or the Great Basin, Brigham Young will actually encourage missionaries amongst Native Americans to take Native American wives. But the earliest interracial marriage that historians are aware of is actually a Native American man and a white woman in Nauvoo, sealed together in Nauvoo.

So [Mormons were] very open in attitude and see a divine destiny of Native Americans and actually believe that Native Americans are going to convert en masse to Mormonism and join with Mormons in ushering in the Millennium. Now really naïve in their vision of this kind of way that they perceive Native Americans to embrace their message because it never happens the way that they had hoped. But nonetheless they do have this vision of uniting with Native Americans and strength in these sort of marginalized groups coming together.

But in the minds of outsiders, that's just evidence that Mormons are attempting to conspire with Native Americans to wipe out the rest of white America. So there are all kinds of really heightened rumors that circulate. Mormons have thousands of Indians at their behest. The Indians are just waiting for the signal from their Mormon overlords to go on the warpath and wipe out the rest of us.

The way that it plays out, Mormons are just sometimes branded as more savage than the savages. They're described sometimes as white Indians, white people who have actually given themselves over to savagery, and because you have denied your racial identity, you actually sink to a level of depravity worse than the Native Americans was the argument, and so Mormons become worse than the Indians whom they go to live amongst, some of the accusations leveled against them.

GT: You had a chapter I know on the Chinese. I guess the Chinese helped build the railroad and at first it seems like Mormons embraced the Chinese, and then I believe it was the 1880s or so they said, well we want to become more white so we'll push the Chinese away. I wonder if you could talk about that.

Paul: Mormons are also conflated with Asians, Muslims, Turks, Chinese. The fear was that Mormons represented a second Oriental problem on American soil. Some actually argue that Mormons will combine with the Chinese immigrants and you have them mixing together and have them creating this, once again, Oriental problem that shines in the face of democracy. Democracy is for the white race, the yellow horde is incapable of democracy.

Mormons are a version of Orientalism because they're practicing polygamy, they're giving their free will over to despots. In all of those ways the argument was that they are more like the Chinese than they are like white Americans, like Anglo-Saxons. Therefore they are suspect.

The same Congress that passes the Chinese Exclusion Act also passes the Edmunds Act and newspapers across the nation argue that America has now solved both Oriental problems. Some of them say, well Chinese should be allowed to stay but the Mormons are the ones that should go, so they are conflated in editorials across the nation with the Chinese problem. There's the Mormon problem, and there's a Chinese problem, and we're trying to solve both Oriental problems at once.

GT: Ok, some people might not be familiar with the Edmunds Act. What was the Edmunds Act?

Paul: The Edmunds Act was a piece of legislation passed in 1882, like I said, the same Congress that passes the Chinese Exclusion Act. They are debating these within a few weeks of each other, which defines a new crime, unlawful cohabitation. The problem up to this point legally, at least in the minds of Congress was that they had outlawed polygamy in 1862, but were not very successful in actually convicting anyone because it's very difficult to prove that a plural marriage has taken place. Mormons aren't leaving paperwork hanging around and so how do you actually prove that there's been a plural marriage that has happened?

Congress in 1882 simply defines a new crime, unlawful cohabitation. No longer then do you then have to prove that a marriage has taken place, you just simply have to prove that a man has unlawfully cohabited with more than one woman. That will lead to the conviction of over 1,000 men and some women and really ratchets up the pressure on the Mormons. So that law passed really quickly in conjunction with the Chinese Exclusion Act, which leads to the conflations of both Oriental problems.

GT: So cohabitation is just a euphemism for sex, right?

Paul: Yeah, or you didn't even have to prove that sex had happened. I mean if a man spends the night with one wife, so the marshals might hang outside of wife #1's house, and then the next night or another time with another wife, that's cohabiting. They didn't have to see sexual relations happening. They just simply have to prove that they're cohabiting.

The Mormon response to this is, well are the marshals following our good senators and congressmen around and finding out, following who they're cohabiting with? Is this being applied equally? Obviously the answer is no. It's being applied exclusively towards the Mormons, but nonetheless that opens up for the prosecution and conviction of Mormons under the unlawful cohabitation.

GT: Huh. That's interesting. So adultery was just fine as long as you were not Mormon.

Paul chuckles: Right, right. Yes.

So in terms of Mormon attitudes towards Asians, that was a part of your question. Very early on, Brigham Young sends missionaries to China and there's just simply a desire to convert them. There's no kind of racial restriction, they're also welcomed in. The problem is they just don't have much success, very little success in the mission to China runs into the Taiping Rebellion so there's political turmoil going on and the missionaries themselves complain. There's the language barrier. There's no one wants to listen to them. They return rather quickly.

There are some converts in Hawaii, also some proselyting efforts amongst Chinese immigrants in California. By the 1880s when you have actual Chinese presence in Utah, Mormons don't really make an effort to missionize amongst them when they're right here. I think by that point, they're fully aware of the way that they've been conflated with the Chinese and I think there's more than an effort for claiming whiteness for themselves. Sometimes that means distancing themselves from the other suspect groups to make the distinction because outsiders are making the conflation so Mormons attempt to create distance.

The Black Mormon Scandals

GT: In some research that I've done on Warner McCary, as I understand it, Warner was, well he claimed to be part Indian, but most people, I believe thought he was black. He actually married the stake president's daughter {pauses}...

Paul: Lucy Stanton

GT: Lucy Stanton, and I believe it was Orson {pauses}...

Paul: I think it was Orson Hyde.

GT: Yes, Orson Hyde married them, as an apostle, so Warner McCary's interesting because he claimed to be, I believe it was Choctaw Indian and he was known as the Lamanite prophet. On the one hand he had blessed Israelite heritage, or at least it was believed—that wasn't true, but on the other hand, a lot of people thought he was black, so you've talked a little bit about amalgamation and how interracial marriage wasn't a problem. Warner was a really interesting person. Are you very familiar with that story?

Paul: Yeah I am. You want me to kind of talk about it?

GT: Sure.

Paul: I'm not completely convinced that Warner is ordained to the priesthood and I know some people have suggested that he is. The only evidence is coming from well outside of anyone who would have been close to what happened. the suggestion is, I think it is Orson Hyde who performs the marriage. I've never been able to verify that marriage taking place at the hands of Orson Hyde, being sealed, or being ordained to the priesthood.

So for me there is still a bit of a question mark there, but regardless, they present themselves as a married couple.

They're in Winter Quarters, [Nebraska] and McCary complains to Brigham Young that he's not being treated well because of his racial identity, so this prompts the meeting between McCary and Lucy Stanton, Brigham Young, and every present member of the Quorum of Twelve Apostles. There are a couple of members who aren't there, but everyone who is at Winter Quarters, and a member of the Quorum of Twelve are in that meeting.

This is really an unprecedented kind of event and the minutes of the meeting really kind of describe McCary in very rambling statements, trying to ferret out his racial identity. He presents himself as a Native American, but like you said, the accusation amongst Mormons in Winter Quarters is that he's black. In fact as best as historians can tell, he's black. He's a former slave, and has this long interview. He also says that he's Adam, the Ancient of Days and he's missing a rib, and so Willard Richards in this meeting kind of examines his body, looks for the missing rib and reports that there's no rib missing. Everything seems to be in place. Brigham Young comes out as McCary is complaining, he says I'm not being treated well because of my racial identity. Some people call me the N-word. What does it matter if I'm Native American or African American or Adam the Ancient of Days? I should be treated well.

Brigham Young really tries to calm him and simply says, we don't care about the color, and he actually refers to Q. Walker Lewis who is another black priesthood holder in Lowell, Massachusetts. He cites him as evidence that Mormons don't care about the color. We have a fine elder, an African in Lowell, Massachusetts he says to McCary in that interview, citing him as evidence that Mormons don't discriminate in terms of priesthood ordination. Brigham

Young goes on record in March 1847 as favorably aware of a black priesthood holder. That's why I think that meeting is so important.

But Brigham Young will leave Winter Quarters. They seem to resolve. McCary leaves the meeting feeling fine about things, but Brigham Young then leads a group into the Great Basin. McCary stays behind in Winter Quarters and actually starts a schismatic group of his own. He's attracting followers and performing sealings to white women in a sexualized ritual that comes to the attention of Parley Pratt who is at Winter Quarters. Pratt will speak out against McCary. Eventually McCary and his followers will be excommunicated. McCary and Lucy Stanton will leave Mormonism and actually reinvent themselves as Native American performers and they perform in all kinds population centers on the East. He describes himself as a Native American prophet and her as his Native American wife even though she's white.

GT: "A Delaware Princess."

Paul agrees: A Delaware Princess, to large audiences. They can never fully escape their racial background. They eventually split. Lucy Stanton will eventually make her way back to Utah Territory, Springville, and reunite with her family but after like 20 years. It's a pretty amazing story.

Brigham Young will return from Great Basin in 1847 and he is met with news of McCary's exploits and race mixing and also news that Enoch Lewis in the Lowell, Massachusetts branch, who is Q. Walker Lewis's son. Enoch Lewis, black married Mary Webster, a white member of the Lowell, Massachusetts branch, and William Appleby, who had been appointed to survey the condition of the branches on the east coast, arrives in Winter Quarters and gives his report to Brigham Young.

Did you know that we have an interracial couple in our branch in Lowell, Massachusetts? Appleby is clearly against race mixing. In his personal diary, he speaks out strongly against it. He records meeting them and said I can't believe that they are members of my church and that we allow this in Mormonism. So he meets with Brigham Young December 3, 1847 and gives his report. There are only 13 lines of that meeting that are recorded and they all center on race mixing. Brigham Young speaks strongly against race mixing, actually advocates capital punishment as the penalty, but he doesn't ever mention priesthood at least in the surviving minutes. The meeting goes on like 4 hours and we've got 13 lines. It's really hard to know the full extent of the conversation but what gets recorded seems to center on Brigham Young, ok I've had enough. We've got McCary who was performing sexualized sealing rituals to white women and then he's met with news of this interracial marriage in Lowell, Massachusetts. He speaks out strongly against it. I think that pushes him in a different direction.

GT: Ok, I guess there's one other important event that I just want to highlight. Are you familiar with Joseph Ball and what happened in Massachusetts as well?

Paul: Yeah so I'm also kind of suspicious of Joseph Ball's racial identity. I've not seen any documents that describe him as black, so I'd like to do some more research on him to try to ferret that out. I'm not quite sure what to make of Joseph Ball yet.

GT: Oh, that's very interesting.

Paul: Yeah. I know that other people have written about Joseph Ball as the first black High Priest and leader in Massachusetts and I'm just kind of waiting to get a chance to try to research that a little bit more and figure out what's going on because it's just odd to me that those who are visiting aren't describing him as black.

GT: Oh really!

Paul: Yeah.

GT: So I guess it's my understanding that he was the first black High Priest and served as branch president there, and I believe it was in Q. Walker Lewis's same branch. Is that right?

Paul: Yeah it was Boston so I'm not sure if it's the same branch or not. It may have been. I'd have to check that out to make sure.

GT: That's my understanding. There was some issues with the branch there with William Smith. Are you familiar with that story?

Paul: Well just maybe the basics. William Smith, who was an apostle, is going to Lowell, Massachusetts and engaging in extramarital sexual exploits. So there's some question about his behavior there and how that kind of impacts his increasingly erratic behavior and his eventual split from Mormonism.

GT: Alright, so let's go back. We've got Warner McCary doing some sexualized sealing rituals with white women, we've got Enoch Lewis with his mixed race child. I've kind of wondered, it seems like this is about the time where Brigham who, in 1846 is impressed with Walker Lewis back in Boston and then in 1852 as he's explaining about slavery, which I want to talk a little bit about slavery being legalized in Utah, that's where he talks about one drop as I recall. Am I telling that right?

Paul: Well if you go with Wilford Woodruff's very truncated attempt at capturing Brigham Young's speech in his journal, then Woodruff will insert the language of one drop into Brigham Young's speech but if you go with George Watt, who captures the speech in Pitman shorthand, George Watt does not have Brigham Young using the one drop language.

GT surprised: Oh! That's an important distinction.

Paul: Yeah.

GT: I know you've warned me about that before and I keep having a problem with that.

Paul chuckles: Yeah. So for the book [Religion of a Different Color] I was able to get back to the Pitman shorthand version of Brigham Young's speeches for the legislative session, and I believe that we shouldn't rely upon Woodruff's very shortened, truncated version. I mean imagine kind of capturing our conversation, trying to capture it in longhand versus a court stenographer trying to capture it. Pitman shorthand isn't as precise as a court stenographer but nonetheless more precise than trying to capture it in longhand and Woodruff captures around 800 words, and Watt captures something like 2400 words, so three times as many, and I think much more precise in capturing what Brigham Young is saying, and Watt does not include the language of one drop, and so in the documentary history we will be producing, we try to make the case that scholars should rely upon the Watt version over the Woodruff version.

GT: I can't tell you how excited I am to see that book.

Becoming a Fanboy of Orson Pratt

GT: I want to jump back to 1840s, 1850s time period. You gave a presentation at Mormon History Association a year or two ago, I don't remember when. I think it was with LaJean Carruth and...

Paul: Christopher Rich.

GT: Christopher Rich. That was a fascinating presentation and I have to tell you that following that presentation, I became a fanboy of Orson Pratt.

Paul chuckles: Uh huh.

GT: I think this is one of the not well-told stories of his opposition to Brigham Young concerning slavery and even black voting which I think would blow most people's minds. Let's talk a little bit more about slavery in Utah. You've got this debate in 1851 I believe in the Utah legislature about whether we should allow slavery in Utah. I believe Charles Rich, one of the apostles in Utah had some slaves, so obviously there were some apostles who wanted to do slavery, but you have Orson Pratt who, it didn't seem like he was in favor of that. Can you talk a little bit about that debate and how it turned out?

Paul: Sure. Orson Pratt gives a speech in opposition to what comes to be called the Servant Code that's being debated by the legislature in 1852. What laws will govern the black slaves who have been brought to Utah Territory by their white slave masters? That's what they're trying to determine in the [18]52 legislative session.

In doing research for the book, I came across these speeches that had never been transcribed from Pitman shorthand and so haven't been a part of historical record as historians have written about these events in the past and the LDS Church History Library was kind enough to have

LaJean Carruth transcribe them and allow me to use them in research for the book.

Orson Pratt gives a speech where he simply speaks out very strongly against the bill the legislature is debating. He speaks out strongly against slavery. He says if the Utah Territory legalizes slavery it will put a black mark on the territory. A variety of countries were emancipating their slaves, outlawing slavery. The British Empire had already done so, obviously the U.S. had not, but Pratt said this will harm our missionary efforts when we go abroad if people become aware that as countries are getting rid of slavery, we're legalizing it. He says we should reject the bill outright and says that if Utah Territory does this the angels of heaven will blush. He's very strong in his notion of why this is wrong.

He argues that curses are not multi-generational, so God may very well curse a people but it's only that people. It doesn't pass down from generation to generation, so he's rejecting the notion of a multigenerational curse might impact if black people truly are the descendants of Cain, that doesn't matter to Orson Pratt because curses are not multigenerational. It would only apply to the generation that God cursed, not to however many generations later, so it's a very singular kind of position he stakes out in Mormonism and ultimately he doesn't win the day but he is speaking out against Brigham Young and they are butting heads in that legislative session.

I think they butt heads again over the election bill, so the election bill is also being debated that legislative session. We know that Orson Pratt speaks February 4th because the evidence within one of Brigham Young's speeches tells us that he does but unfortunately that speech is not recorded. We'd love to know what Orson Pratt says on February 4th because Brigham Young will say on February 4th, no one got up to speak until Pratt got up to speak and he only got up to speak to stick his thumb me. So we know that Pratt spoke on February 4th and we know that he was aiming at Brigham Young because Brigham Young tells us that that's the case. Then Brigham Young, and they're debating the election bill. Who's going to be able to vote in the Utah Territory?

GT: Let me just interrupt you for a second. So Brigham Young at the time was serving as governor in Utah. What was Pratt's position?

Paul: So Brigham Young is serving as prophet as well as governor, and Pratt is serving as apostle as well as legislator. So you have these obviously mixed roles taking place and they're butting heads. They've butted heads before, they'll butt heads again, but they're diametrically opposed in this legislative session.

Brigham Young will give a speech the morning of 5th of February and it's his most fully articulated race-based priesthood restriction but it also is really helpful to know that he's arguing about the election bill because within that race-based priesthood restriction, he's simply saying blacks will not rule over me in Utah Territory, so we're not going to give them the right to vote and they will not rule over me in this church. We're not going to give them the priesthood, so those are the positions that he's staking out and I really believe that he is speaking in opposition to Orson Pratt's speech February 4th, the day before. We don't have the speech, but when Brigham Young says in his 5th of February speech, if no other prophet said it before now, I say it. Black people are the descendants of old Cain and are barred from the priesthood. He actually says he's striking out on his own that if no other prophet said it before, I'm saying it now. So I am starting a new trajectory. I'm distinguishing myself and when I hear him say that I imagine Orson Pratt the day before saying, no other prophet said this before, and this is Brigham Young's response: Well if no one ever said it before, I'm saying it now! That's the context.

Obviously I can't prove it because we don't have Pratt's speech but I imagine that Brigham Young is obviously speaking to Pratt, and we know that in the context of the speech that he did in fact he is. We know that Pratt spoke the day before and they are in a heated debate, so how does Pratt push back? The minutes of the legislature tell us that that afternoon of February 5th, after Brigham Young has given this very strong speech, there are two bills that are introduced that are just innocuous bills, like who cares? It's the Cedar City and Fillmore municipal bills where they're just approving them as legal municipal entities, but within the bills are the voting rights for Fillmore and Cedar City. Who gets to vote in Fillmore and Cedar City? They stipulate that white men over 21 get to vote, and that's par for the course for the nation in 1852.

Pratt votes against both of those bills and the minutes tell us that he does so because they don't allow black men to vote and I believe that's his effort at again, pushing back against Brigham Young, so Brigham Young got to have his say in the morning and this is Pratt's way of responding. I'm going to vote against these two municipal bills to make my point that I believe black men should be allowed to vote in Utah Territory.

GT: To me that is absolutely astonishing because this is the year 1852. This is pre-Civil War.

Paul: That's right.

GT: I mean how did Pratt fit in with the rest of America as far as a black man should be allowed to vote because I can't imagine that's a popular position?

Paul: It's really not. I mean there are a few people who are arguing for this, you know radical abolitionists but like I said this is just a radical minority. To stake out that kind of position, you would be branded as a radical minority, marginalized from the mainstream. It really is kind of a distinct position and for him to be making it in Utah Territory really is quite unique for 1852. Not many are advocating for black suffrage in 1852.

GT: I mean when were blacks allowed to vote?

Paul: Well remember you have the 15th Amendment which is passed following the Civil War and I don't remember. [chuckles] That's going to make me look bad. I don't remember what year that's actually ratified, but it's one of the three amendments that come out of the Civil War, the 13th Amendment eradicates slavery, 14th Amendment Civil Rights, and then the 15th Amendment is black suffrage.

GT: So 1860s, 1870s?

Paul: Yeah. Exactly.

GT: That's good enough. But even still blacks still have the problem with voting because we still have the 1962 Voting Rights Act.

Paul: Right.

GT: Can you just fill me in there? What was going on in that 80 years or whatever?

Paul: Sure, so Reconstruction. How do you put the nation back together sort of dominates American politics after the Civil War and you have radical Republicans in Congress who are in favor of black suffrage and that is finally passed with the 15th Amendment and there is a period of time where blacks enjoy that right to vote and you have the first black senator is elected to the United States Senate during that Reconstruction period.

But then there's going to be the backlash in the South, the reassertion of white supremacy and the KKK becomes really the paramilitary arm of the Democratic Party, and if you vote the Republican ticket you're subject to intimidation by the KKK, you're subject to violence and subject to death, especially black people. So in essence the KKK and then black codes that start to be written, poll taxes, a variety of ways, literacy tests start to be incorporated in the South, strip that right away from blacks in the South.

You have Plessy vs. Ferguson in 1896, black codes being written across the South. Obviously federal troops are all withdrawn from the South in 1877 so as historians we see that as the end of the Reconstruction Era and when the troops are gone, you have no one left to enforce the laws that have been passed, so southern whites just simply regain white supremacy, regain control, segregate blacks in every way possible, strip rights that were granted to them as a result of the 14th and 15th Amendments, strip them from them and you have the Supreme Court that puts its stamp of approval on that in Plessy vs. Ferguson in 1896 and so racial segregation then takes over and therefore you need the Civil Rights Movement in the 1950s and '60s and the Voting Rights Act and the Civil Rights Act in the 1960s as a result.

GT: Wow. That's great. So going back to Orson Pratt like I said there, I am just so amazed that in 1852 he is making such an amazing thing. From what I understand, this speech has not been known until a year or two ago, is that correct?

Paul: That's correct.

GT: At least among historians.

Paul: That's right, that's right because George Watt never did transcribe it himself so it stayed in his papers only in Pitman shorthand form and there are a few people left on the planet that can read Pitman shorthand and one of them works for the LDS Church History Library, LaJean Carruth and she's been going through a lot of these Pitman speeches and transcribing them but it takes a long time, and it was only when I made a request for my book to see if there was a Pitman shorthand version of Brigham Young's speech, because I wanted to get as close to his original words as possible that it led to the discovery of these other speeches from the legislative session.

GT: Wow. So do you wish Orson Pratt was more well known among modern Mormons?

Paul: Well of course for that speech especially. I mean obviously there may be some things Orson Pratt did and said that might cause us pause but {Paul chuckles} certainly the position that he stakes out in 1852, I wish that was more well-known and that really Brigham Young's position comes out of a debate with Orson Pratt over a legislative bill. This is not sort of a context that believing Latter-day Saints would suggest is conducive for revelation, that Brigham Young is sort of experiencing some sort of divine intervention here, but in fact he's engaging in a debate with an apostle legislator and he is articulating his most forceful position on a racial priesthood restriction in that debate.

GT: Like I said I am just so amazed. I think that's one of the coolest episodes of Mormon history I've ever heard!

Paul chuckles: Yeah!

Dating the LDS Temple and Priesthood Ban

GT: Do you know when approximately that time was where they went from embracing other religious and ethnic minorities to pushing them away?

Paul: Yeah it's sort of just gradual across the course of the 19th century. I mean the most evidence is with blacks and so at least two black men are ordained to the Melchizedek Priesthood in the first couple of decades of Mormonism and then you see sort of that deterioration across the course of the 19th century in fits and starts, right? Brigham Young first openly articulates the race-based priesthood restriction in 1852 but I don't it's really actually lock-step in place until 1908 with Joseph F. Smith and you have a lot of intervening kind of events that it takes on a life of its own, accumulates precedent in each succeeding leadership group not willing to violate the precedent established by the previous group even though Brigham Young's position is a violation of a precedent that Joseph Smith established of open priesthood ordination.

But after Brigham Young articulates a race-based priesthood restriction, then it grows to a race-based temple restriction. The leadership by the 1880s, they're remembering back, well I remember Brigham Young said this, and some actually saying well I think Joseph Smith said it or it began with Joseph Smith and the last brick is in place in 1908 when the black priesthood holders are erased from collective Mormon memory. Joseph F. Smith in a 1908 meeting will simply say that Joseph Smith himself declared Elijah Abel, a black priesthood holder's ordination null and void himself. There's no evidence that that's true, but he's falsely remembering back in 1908. So once you have that as a new memory, like you've erased the black

Mormon priesthood holders from collective Mormon memory, the new memory moving forward then is that this restriction has always been in place, it was there from the beginning, Joseph Smith began it, we can't do anything about it, it's going to take a revelation to get rid of it, and I think that transition takes place in 1908.

That very same meeting Joseph F. Smith will say that missionaries should no longer proselyte amongst black people, that if they want to get baptized, it's going to be of their own volition but missionaries shouldn't actively go out seeking converts amongst them, which is absolutely a very different perspective then animated the early years of Mormonism where missionaries were preaching in all groups.

There's a letter from the president of the Northern States Mission in the 19-teens, I can't remember the exact year and it simply says we have three black families in the Northern States mission. There's one in Wisconsin, there's one in Indiana, there's one in Minnesota. The problem is when our missionaries bring white investigators to these congregations they are repelled. They say well that we don't want to worship with black people, and so I have instructed my missionaries to stop proselyting in black neighborhoods. So that's how Mormonism is known and branded as a white church. They stop actively proselyting amongst black people because by that point remember the Supreme Court has put its stamp of approval on segregation, on separate but equal. You have white investigators showing up to these congregations seeing black families, and they're saying, oh it's those people should be segregated. We don't want to worship with them. It's deemed by the mission president in the Northern States Mission as too problematic, so his solution is he tells his missionaries to stop proselyting in black neighborhoods.

GT: That's interesting. I've had a debate with a few other people about, when did the ban actually start? It's interesting, you've taken the opposite position of me. To me it looks like, from my research it looks like the last person ordained, the last black man ordained was 1846 Warner McCary in Nauvoo. I believe it was Orson Pratt or Orson Hyde, I don't remember but no one was ordained after that and so I guess you can call that period from 1846-1908 as kind of a de facto ban maybe. {Paul nods} I actually did want to get into 1852 as well.

Paul nods: Sure.

GT: We can talk about that. Would you agree that there was kind of a de facto ban because Warner McCary, he was a colorful person, maybe you could talk a little bit about him.

Paul: Sure. Yeah so to be clear what I'm saying is they aren't actively ordaining men to the priesthood at least as much as they are aware during that time period but it's still not completely solidified in my estimation, like the last brick in this wall of racial restriction, so I see it accumulating bricks across the course of 19th century. The last brick is 1908 when you erase from collective Mormon memory Elijah Abel as a black priesthood holder.

There's a meeting in 1879 when Elijah Abel appeals to be sealed to his wife and to have his endowment, so I suggest then in the book [Religion of a Different Color], which touches off an investigation. John Taylor who's been the leader of Mormonism leads this investigation. If the racial restriction is unambiguously in place as late as 1879, why do you need to have an investigation? If it's completely understood and everyone's on board, why investigate? That's 1879. As late as 1879 there are questions about what do we do when Elijah Abel wants to be sealed to his wife and get his endowment?

Joseph F. Smith is sent to meet with Elijah Abel and comes back to report that Abel has produced priesthood certificates and says that Joseph Smith himself sanctioned his priesthood. Joseph F. Smith reports that in that meeting. The decision is that they will allow his priesthood to stand but not allow him temple admission so you have then this accumulating precedent and then and really then the beginning of the temple restriction that grows out of this priesthood ban. But Abel goes on another mission and dies with his priesthood intact and his son and grandson are also ordained, so there are exceptions.

GT: Do you know when his son and grandson were ordained, approximately what years?

Paul: Yeah, so I think the son, oh it's in the book. I think the son is the 19-teens, I think it's 1912 and the grandson 1935, both of them in Logan.

GT: So even after the final brick we still have some exceptions?

Paul: Yes, that's exactly right. That's exactly right.

In 1907 the First Presidency puts the one drop rule into play which simply stipulates that anyone with one drop of African ancestry cannot hold the priesthood or be admitted into the temple, and that's typical of what's going on in the nation so states like Virginia are adopting the one drop rule define legally, who is black and who is white, and Virginia says if you have one drop of black ancestry, then according to the law of the state of Virginia, you are legally black. You can have 100 white ancestors and one black ancestor and you would still be defined legally as black.

The same thing then that the First Presidency articulates in 1907 for priesthood and temple admission is the one drop policy, so that's a policy impossible to enforce. We know now especially with DNA, so there are all kinds of exceptions if the one drop rule is the standard, all kinds of exceptions that make it through a wall that becomes impossible to police.

Dr. Reeve: How These Race Lessons Apply Today

GT: Let's move on. I've already taken way more time than I said I was going to. I just want to kind of finish up and bring us more to modern day. I believe it was 2012, 2013 the LDS Church came out a new Race essay. Some think that it went too far in blaming Brigham Young for the ban. Some people think it didn't go far enough. It didn't apologize for the ban or state explicitly—it kind of hints at, well there were a lot of other explanations but just ignore them. They weren't correct. But they don't talk about what they were, the Curse of Cain, the Curse of Ham. So where do you fit on that. What do you think?

Paul: Yeah I think that it's probably—well I guess for me the LDS Church does not issue a major disavowal that frequently, so it disavows previous teachings. That doesn't happen very often. In my estimation it's a pretty big step and it also includes the condemnation of all racism past and present, and that includes within Mormonism. There's a condemnation of racism and a major disavowal of black skin being a curse, of interracial marriage as a sin, of blacks or any other ethnic or racial group as being inferior in any sort of way whatsoever to anyone else, and so in my estimation those are really important steps forward, actually a major step forward. It was approved by the First Presidency and the Quorum of the Twelve.

Certainly some people would want more. It stops short of arguing one way or the other as to if the racial restriction was of divine origins or of human origins but certainly gives the impression that it grew out of simply a racial culture, not out of divine origins. All of those things considered I think it was pretty dramatic step.

GT: I believe it was in the 1980s, 1981 if I remember right, Ronald Esplin, he's a church historian, came out with an essay kind of refuting Lester Bush's 1973 essay in which Lester tried to pin the beginnings of the ban about 1847, and it seems to be when Parley P. Pratt was speaking against Warner McCary. Esplin tried to push it back to possibly some secret temple teachings. It seems as I recall there were some people that still want to pin the ban back on Joseph Smith. Number one are you familiar with that and have you talked to Ron Esplin to see how he feels about that.

Paul: I have not personally talked to Ron. I am familiar with his article. I just don't buy the argument in the article. You know he seems to suggest that Brigham Young didn't do anything that Joseph Smith didn't first do, and you simply have to have evidence. At least to date there is no existing evidence of Joseph Smith articulating a race-based priesthood restriction or a race-based temple restriction. In fact the evidence suggests otherwise.

Elijah Abel actually says that Joseph Smith sanctions his priesthood. He was ordained an elder. We don't know who ordained him an elder in March of 1836 but there is a certificate that survives with Joseph Smith's signature on it which defines Elijah Abel as an ordained minister, ordained and able to preach the Mormon gospel, articulates his priesthood as an elder. It's not his ordination certificate but it is a certificate signed by Joseph Smith where Joseph Smith's signature is saying that yes Elijah Abel is a minister representing Mormonism.

GT: Would that be similar to how a missionary card today that missionaries carry around?

Paul: Yes, that's exactly right. Elijah Abel when he's interviewed by Joseph F. Smith in 1879 says Joseph Smith sanctioned my priesthood. The evidence is contrary to any suggestion that Joseph Smith began a priesthood restriction, so we have no statements by Joseph Smith articulating a race-based priesthood restriction. Historians just have to follow the evidence and I just don't see the evidence. I mean you can't just sort of simply surmise that in my estimation that Brigham Young never did anything like Joseph Smith didn't at least initiate at first.

The other point that's really important for me at least in putting the pieces together is that Brigham Young in on record in 1847 as favorably aware of Q. Walker Lewis's priesthood, and then in his speech on 5th of February 1852 he says *if no other prophet ever said it before me, I say it now*, where he also seems to be striking out on his own!

So all of those together in my estimation put the priesthood restriction at the feet of Brigham Young as beginning it; we don't have evidence that Joseph Smith did, but we do have evidence that Brigham Young is forcefully stating that he is the first who's prophet stating it.

GT: Very good. Now I want to ask you another question. I'm hoping you'll answer. I've heard rumors, and that's all they are is rumors that you played a role in compiling that essay [Race and the Priesthood]. Do you have any response to that?

Paul laughs: I did help with the essay. Yeah, Yeah.

GT: So was it, can you describe your role?

Paul: Well the Church History Department invited me to write an extended essay. It ended up being about 55 pages long with footnotes and everything like I would produce as an academic essay. Once they were satisfied with that it was sent up the line, several layers of approval process and then the Church History Department actually boiled down that longer essay to what got posted online so I had no say over what got posted online, what eventually appeared as Race and the Priesthood, but it was a condensed version of the longer piece that I produced for them.

GT: Very much condensed if it was 55 pages, now it's what 3-4 pages?

Paul: Yeah I think it prints out at with the footnotes at like 8 pages at LDS.org, so very much condensed but the fuller essay was sent up the line and then it was out of my hands after that and they condensed it down to what was published at LDS.org

GT: Well that's cool. Great. I'll have to get a copy of that 55 page paper!

Paul laughs: They have that in their control but actually the 55 pages are basically a boiled down version of the four chapters in the book.

GT: Oh, Ok.

Paul: Yeah. So the Church History Department was aware that I was doing research on this topic and invited me to participate and the 55 pages like I said are basically a condensed version of the four chapters and I got to say whatever I wanted in the four chapters in the book because it's published by Oxford and there are obviously no restrictions there so if you want sort of the full version, you can look at those four chapters in the book

GT: Well I have to tell you I highly recommend that book. That's an awesome, awesome book.

Paul: Thank you.

GT: Well done. Do you think the Church will ever apologize for the ban?

Paul: I, um, I doubt it. I'm kind of skeptical that they will, but you know it's hard to predict the future and what the next generation of leadership might look like and how attitudes may change over time but I don't see this generation of leaders apologizing. The statement doesn't apologize, right? But it does disavow and it does condemn. I think that's probably as far as they were willing to go at this point.

GT: I know some historians have likened the ban on blacks to the current ban on gays within the church. Do you see these as similar or is there significant difference?

Paul: Well I guess there are ways in which I could see them as similar and ways in which I think they're distinct. The similarities could be that, is this simply the sort of cultural context, right? That is somehow seeping in, it would be hard to argue that the cultural context of America moving towards legalizing gay marriage didn't impact Mormonism, right? So it's Mormonism responding to its cultural context the same way that Mormonism seemed to respond to the racial context in the 19th century, so a parallel there, but I think also important distinctions.

So for race and priesthood in particular there is an historical precedent, right? Black men were ordained to the priesthood in the early decades of Mormonism and I'm not aware of a precedent for gay marriage in the early decades of Mormonism. Then the other important distinction is that black people in Mormonism were the only group prevented from having all of the saving rituals that Mormonism requires for the Mormon heaven. You can be gay and receive all of the saving ordinances that Mormonism requires, and so black people are the only group that I'm aware of that were ever prevented from receiving all of the saving ordinances so it's not the same kind of pressure point.

Now I realize that gay Latter-day Saints like gay marriage as a part of that process, but nonetheless they're not barred from receiving the Endowment, they are not barred from temple participation like black people were. Black people were prevented from receiving all the saving ordinances and the same thing for female priesthood ordination, right? You could make the same kind of case that it's not necessary for saving ordinances and so it's not the same kind of issue as it was with black Latter-day Saints who were only allowed to receive the Gift of the Holy Ghost but were prevented from receiving the other saving ordinances that Mormonism defines as necessary for exaltation. So that's the only case I'm aware of that comes in to impact.

Now if we talk about the more recent marriage policy, we're talking about children of gay couples who are being prevented from those saving ordinances, there may be a new parallel there, right? Being prevented from the saving ordinances, not of your own volition but simply because your parents are in a gay marriage, so that's the first time that I see us returning back, or Mormonism returning back to something, that they had prevented a group, in this case black Latter-day Saints from receiving all the saving ordinances and now they're preventing—and not because of their own sins, right? Not because of worthiness but because of Cain killing Abel, and in this case once again gay parents, children of gay parents not because of their own choices but because of their parents' choices. So that is a parallel that I see that wasn't in existence before the most recent policy came into play.

GT: That brings up another point. I know that immediately after the announcement, the November 2015 Announcement I believe it was, where they prevented children of gay parents from being ordained, baptism, or whatever, I know a lot of people came out with the Second Article of Faith as Orson Pratt did in the Legislature: "Men should be punished for their own sins and not for Adam's transgression."

I'll tell you what, I've had some debates online about whether, does God punish as Orson Pratt said, only this generation, or does He punish future generations through not allowing ordinances. Some people say well God's cursed lots of people and you can read the Bible. There's lots of curses in the Bible that are supposedly from God, or the prophets claim are from God. So how do you interpret? I guess I'm putting on your theologian hat on there.

Paul: Yeah.

GT: But how do you feel about that, especially with regards to the Second Article of Faith?

Paul: Sure, so my understanding of curse is not something that God distributes but in fact that a person may curse themselves as a separation from God and it's through the person's actions and that can be overcome simply through repentance. So I see that as how curses are supposed to operate. It's not how Brigham Young articulated it and Orson Pratt, as you note, pushes back against it and I see it as a violation of the Second Article of Faith. Absolutely, I see the position that Brigham Young staked out in 1852 as a violation of the Second Article of Faith. He's holding all black people accountable for Cain's murder of Abel, something they did not participate in. That's a violation of the principle Joseph Smith establishes in the Second Article of Faith, and I see then the November 5th policy also as a violation of that Second Article of Faith. Holding children of gay couples accountable for decisions they are not making themselves.

Yeah. So I absolutely see it as a violation of the Second Article of Faith.

GT: Great, one other parallel I just wanted to point out. You mentioned the one drop rule, that there were probably lots of people with more than one drop of blood who were ordained but they looked white. With the gays, there have been lots of gays ordained, not openly. Maybe they got married in the temple or whatever, got the priesthood as they should have done at certain ages, but then came out as gay after, and now they have priesthood. So it's kind of interesting to me, it seems like we're reverting back to the days of Brigham Young. We're trying to prevent this, but it's an impossible thing to prevent. What are your thoughts on that?

Paul: Well yeah, I mean a person even could be openly gay and hold the priesthood and be ordained to the priesthood as long as they are adhering to what the Church articulates as its Law of Chastity, right? So you can openly identify as gay and still be ordained to the priesthood so that's a way in which it's a distinction or a difference from how the racial priesthood restriction operated.

But you're right in terms of a person's sexual identity and if they're open about it or not open about it and being ordained to the priesthood happening regardless of whether they're open or not open about it. So it is like the one drop rule. It's impossible to police. Trying to police someone's sexual identity is also very problematic as well.

GT: Ok, well I'm just going to ask you one last question and I'll let you go. You know the Tabernacle Choir is going to be singing here at the inauguration of soon to be President Trump. {Note this was recorded Jan 18, 2017, just 2 days prior to inauguration} A lot of people, I would expect Orson Pratt probably wouldn't think that would be a good idea.

Paul laughs.

GT: What are your thoughts about—President Trump has been very vocal about race and not in a way that I don't think Mormons are comfortable with. He got the lowest vote total of any Republican in Utah in decades, probably since Roosevelt I believe or maybe [Lyndon] Johnson [in 1963]. But what are your thoughts about the Church sending the choir to President Trump's inauguration?

Paul: You're hitting all the hot button issues, you're not letting me off easy here! [chuckles] I would prefer that the Tabernacle Choir not go. I just think as much distance from Donald Trump as possible is a good thing, even if we were to talk about simple religious pluralism and religious freedom. It's a position that the Church has staked out for itself, and it has always strongly advocated for religious liberty, religious freedom, and you have a president who is arguing for a Muslim ban on immigration and also suggested Muslim surveillance, a Muslim registry, those type of things that are just absolutely shining in the face of religious liberty and if that was the only principle that they wanted to stand on, I would love for them to stand on that principle. When Trump first articulated his position on a Muslim ban, the LDS Newsroom did issue statement where they cited Joseph Smith's position in Nauvoo welcoming Muslims and so they did speak out then but the fact that the choir is going just seems like too close of an association with a president who has staked out positions on race, on religious liberty and his actual attitude towards women, those kind of things just really kind of shine in the face of fundamental Mormon principles.

So it's just a personal opinion. I would rather they not go. Just stay as far away from--Mormonism teaches its adherents "stay away from the edge." Don't muddy the water. Don't flirt with evil, those kind of things and so for me, that's a principle that's at play here. I know other people have articulated other Mormon principles that they believe is at play and actually suggest that that's a reason for the Mormon Tabernacle Choir to perform. To me it doesn't outweigh the reasons not to perform, so my personal position is I wish they weren't going, but I don't get to make those decisions.

GT: Alright, well thank you so much for your time. Like I said I know I took way longer than I told you I would so it's been a pleasure. I hope that you're open to another interview, maybe the Mountain Meadows Massacre or some benign topic like that.

Paul laughs: Yes! We can cover all the other hot button issues.

GT: Alright, well once again thank you Paul Reeve. I really appreciate your time here on Gospel Tangents!

Paul: Oh thank you!

Epilogue

I really appreciate Paul for taking time to talk with us and hope you learned as much as I did. Black History Month is over so we'll end the month talking about the first documented former slave to join the Church. He's known in Mormon Journals as "Black Pete" and Dr. Mark Staker of the Church History Library tells us about his conversion to the Church of Christ in November 1830, about six months after the church was organized in New York. Black Pete lived in Kirtland, Ohio.

Mark: Mormon missionaries baptized most of the members of the Morley family and Black Pete participates in all this, he's preaching and helping with baptisms later on so we have to assume he's baptized and that he's ordained a priest as well.

I hope you'll tune in for our next conversation with Dr. Staker! For more information, please subscribe to our website https://GospelTangents.com where you can purchase a transcript of this podcast for just $3. You can also get one at Amazon.com. Please subscribe to iTunes, Stitcher, or YouTube to get updated interviews. Thanks again for listening, and we hope you'll continue to support us here at Gospel Tangents!

Additional Resources:

Here are links to the blog so you can join the conversation, as well as videos of the interview.

Part 1: How Mormons Became a Racial Category
Video: https://www.youtube.com/watch?v=5kTPLAW8kZ8&t

Part 2: How Did Others Deal with Slavery?
Video: https://www.youtube.com/watch?v=sUrZs8dDHqA&t

Part 3: What were Joseph Smith's views on Muslims, Chinese, and Indians?
Video: https://www.youtube.com/watch?v=vxmyIlilaoc

Part 4: The Black Mormon Scandals
Video: https://www.youtube.com/watch?v=W9idYUEocFg

Part 5: Becoming a Fanboy of Orson Pratt

Part 6: Dating the LDS Temple and Priesthood Ban
Video: https://www.youtube.com/watch?v=aLToEVzr8eA

Part 7: Dr Reeve: Applying these Race Lessons Today

To learn more about how race affects Mormons, both past and present, check out Paul's book:

Religion of a Different Color

Paul has some other books as well.

Mormonism: A Historical Encyclopedia

Mormons, Miners, and Southern Paiutes

Between Pulpit and Pew: The Supernatural World in Mormon History and Folklore

Paul's other books can be found on his Author Page.

Given the new Executive Order banning Muslims from entering the United States, I wanted to share Paul Reeve's Op Ed in the Deseret News – My view: Trump's Muslim ban looks like Mormon ban

You may be interested in our interviews with Margaret Young:

Part 1: Biography of Jane Manning James (Jane was a black Mormon pioneer that knew Joseph Smith well)

Part 2: Race is a Touchy Subject (Margaret's experiences trying to promote play about Jane's life)

We'd also love to have you visit our Amazon Store on our website to see other books on Black LDS History, and other Mormon topics. Be sure to check out our blog as well at https://GospelTangents.com to find information about future guests and projects we are working on. We would also like to partner with artists and musicians to produce a documentary on this and other topics. Please email us at GospelTangents@gmail.com if you're interested.

Thank you for your generous support!

www.ingramcontent.com/pod-product-compliance
Lightning Source LLC
Chambersburg PA
CBHW050517290526
45786CB00007B/2596